THE COLLEGE TRAP

What Colleges Don't Tell You!
What You Need to Know.

JAMES W. WILCOX, JR.

Wasteland Press

www.wastelandpress.net
Shelbyville, KY USA

The College Trap:
What Colleges Don't Tell You! What You Need to Know.
by James W. Wilcox, Jr.

First Printing – January 2019
Paperback ISBN: 978-1-68111-279-4

Printed in the U.S.A.

0   1   2   3

ACKNOWLEDGMENTS

In Humble Gratitude, I want to thank God for allowing me to write this book to help others start their educational journey. I want to thank my family for investing in me, without you, none of this would be possible. To ALL my teachers for investing time and energy in me, eternal gratitude. Sending soulful shout outs to Norfolk State University, United Theological Seminary, and Florida Memorial University, and my classmates there that have impacted my life in so many ways. Thank you to the "Ride or Lives," my YouTube family. Lastly, showing how college experiences can lead to amazing lifelong college friendships, to my Editor, Anissa D. Christopher, my Fellow Spartan and Alumna thank you for putting the Spartan stamp of approval on it before publishing. Finally, I would like to thank the Supporters and readers of this book, thank all of you.

TABLE OF CONTENTS

INTRODUCTION

According to the Association for College Admission Counseling (2015), the average American high school has one guidance counselor for 500 students. Looking at this statistic, do you think your child is getting all the college advising he or she needs? Do you want to take a chance and hope the counselor will help your child? If you answered no to any of these questions, then this book is for you!

As a former Academic Dean for Strayer University, I was alarmed at how many students did not know about accreditation. No one had ever talked to them about early college programs or even taking courses before stepping foot on a college campus. I grew weary of students saying that they wish they would have talked to me before they enrolled at certain colleges.

I was angered by how colleges took advantage of low-income and first-generation college students. Many of these students trusted admissions officers. However, little did they know that they were just a meal-ticket and a salary increase for a dishonest admissions counselor.

I also had to look back at my academic journey. I learned many lessons along the way. I attended a college in Kansas because they gave me a full-tuition scholarship, but it was not a social or academic fit for me. I transferred to another college, losing time as well as college credits. Had someone counseled me, I may have completed my studies on time.

After witnessing these types of events happening repeatedly to numerous students, I asked myself; what can I do to help these students? The answer was, to write a book and start to educate first-generation students, their parents, and adult learners. No one should feel that that they have been exploited. I hope that the information in this book saves you time and money.

This is a short book, but it is packed with vital information! I made sure to provide links to the resources mentioned in this book. **Please use them**! Also, if you care to use my academic advising services, please visit my webpage at: www.simplycollege.net.

CHAPTER ONE:

Why I Wrote This Small Book

As a high school senior, I had no idea what my plans were after graduation. My mother and father were not college graduates. My sisters only attended the local community college, and I really did not seriously start to think about college until the last month before graduation. I was fortunate that I selected a regionally accredited community college. Afterwards, I transferred to a private regionally accredited college. Finally, I matriculated and graduated from a regionally accredited state university.

My numerous college transfers caused me to miss my 1992 college graduation date. However, I took it in stride and graduated in 1993. Even though I *thought* I was just an average college student, eventually, I graduated with four advanced degrees.

Later, in my professional life, I became an Academic Dean for a reputable for-profit university. You will understand later in the book why I chose the word "reputable." During this time, I realized that many students were not getting the assistance they needed in navigating the college admissions process in high school. Many of these students were first-generation, low-income, or working-class students. I also noticed that many adult learners were not knowledgeable about the college process either.

After seeing students saddled with debt, choosing schools that were not a good fit for them, and selecting institutions with bad reputations, I decided that I could help individuals planning to attend college with this how-to book.

Before you read any further, I want you to know that this book is very simple; it will be a guide to help you through your college process. I did not want to load this book full of useless information, but instead, with general short tips to help you navigate through your college process. Most of the information comes from my own experience of being a College Dean and Student Support Director. However, occasionally, you will get cited information from other experts in the field.

This book is for high school students planning to attend college, adult learners who have never attended college, or for those who did not complete the college process. This book is for the parents of high school students who do not know where to start. This book is also for stressed out high school guidance counselors.

In short, if you have an interest in higher learning, this book is for you. If this book has been helpful by saving you money, helping you avoid a degree-mill, helping you chose the right college, or any other reason you can think of, please let me know. My e-mail can be found near the back of this publication.

CHAPTER TWO:

You Have to Prepare for College!

To prepare for college, you **need** to know what courses you should be taking in high school. This chart shows what my recommendations are for the average high school student planning to attend college.

English 4 Units	Composition	American Lit.	English Lit.	World Lit.	Rhetoric
Math 3 or 4 Units (depending on the college)	Algebra/Not Pre-Algebra	Geometry	Trigono-metry	Other Advanced Math	
Social Studies 3 Units	U.S. History	World History	Geography	Government	Economics /Law
Natural Sciences 3 Units	Biology	Chemistry	Physical Science	Take At Least 2 Labs	

Go online to verify the college's course requirements. Some colleges may require additional courses. This is one reason why parents should start talking about college with their children **before** they start high school. If there is a college that the student has in mind, the student and the parents should start looking at the course requirements. This is critical in the college admission process. This process should start in the student's **first** year of high school.

Parents, it is important to invest in your child's learning. Before a student attends high school, it is critical that the student's strengths and weaknesses are identified early, starting with elementary continuing into middle school. Parents should work with the student's instructors and seek outside help to tutor the student. In my experience, most students struggle with English or math, oftentimes, it is both subjects.

If you are on a tight budget, I would recommend that you use www.khanacamdemy.com, you can also find Khan Academy on YouTube. For history, religion and social studies, try using the **"Crash Course Channel,"** on YouTube. I do not recommend that you put the student in courses that are not college-preparatory. Colleges look very closely at the courses the student has taken in high school.

Things to Remember
- Make sure to review your child's courses to see if they match the university requirements.
- Do not take "easy" core courses (English, Math, and Science) if you are planning to attend college.

- Do your best to get into AP and IB (Advance Placement and International Baccalaureate) courses. Try even harder to get into early college or dual enrollment programs.

- If you are struggling in a subject, ask for help from the teacher or seek outside assistance.

- Visit with your guidance counselor and make sure things are on schedule. Stick to the program!

What Your Child Should Be Doing
In Each High School Grade Level.

Freshman:	Take Challenging Courses. Avoid easier Courses.	Meet with your counselor twice a year.	Talk to an advisor or counselor about AP Advance Placement courses honor courses, and IB (International Baccalaureate programs.	Get involved with community and leadership organizations.	Start thinking about what you may want to do for a career. Research what courses you will need, the demand for the job, and the pay scale.	Take notes of accomplish-ments, save awards, and honors. Prepare a bio or resume of your achievements.
Sophomore:	Attend college fairs.	Prepare and take the practice PSAT test.	Reach out to a mentor in your area of interest.	Start to research colleges online.	Start looking at funding options.	
Junior:

Fall | Take the PSAT test. (This is needed for many national and merit scholarships.) | Continue to research colleges. | Continue to do research on careers that interest you. | | | |

Junior: Spring	Register for the ACT or SAT/Take practice test.	Start thinking about how you will pay for college.	Start to inquire about scholarships and their application deadline.	Reach out to colleges for information and applications.		
Senior:	Start college visits.	Narrow down college choices.	Make decision on early admissions programs.	Enter and update information in FAFSA. https://student aid.ed.gov/sa/fafsa	Register for and take (or retake) the SAT and/or ACT, if not already done.	Complete and submit scholarship applications prior to deadlines.
Senior:	Consider college acceptances; compare financial aid packages offered.	Make informed decisions about student loans.	Complete and submit scholarship applications prior to deadlines.	Request transcripts and letters of recommendation.	Register for a Federal Student Aid PIN.	Meet with a counselor to verify that graduation requirements will be met on schedule.

CHAPTER THREE:

Ways to Take College Courses Before Going to College

P arents and students, the name of the "college game," is to take as many college courses as you can **before** arriving to college. This will give you "Academic Currency." I will explain the meaning of "Academic Currency" in chapter 9. This does a few things for you. First, it will save you a great deal of money. Secondly, it may shorten your time in college. Thirdly, it demonstrates to the college or university that you can handle college courses, and finally, it will determine your academic strengths and weaknesses. You will need to have this information to select the right college to cater to your needs.

Starting with 9th grade and beyond, your high school and college transcripts are like a "credit score." More difficult courses, along with higher grades, places you in better standing. Colleges are willing to risk admitting you if you have proven that you can successfully pass college courses. The more college courses you take before arriving to college, in my opinion, the better chance you will have of getting admitted. Please understand that your test scores, Grade Point Average, college essays, along with volunteering and extra-curricular activities, all factor into your admissions process.

Please note, all college admissions processes are not created equally, some colleges are very selective, while others may have an open admissions policy. Nevertheless, you want to do your very best, so you can have a variety of options. I am going to briefly explain six options that will allow you to take college courses before you step foot on a college campus. I am sure there are more ways to earn college credits, but these six are a great start.

Advance Placement, or AP Courses
https://apstudent.collegeboard.org/home

So, what are AP courses? AP courses are rigorous, college-level courses in a variety of subjects that give students an opportunity to gain the skills and experience colleges recognize (The College Board, 2012).

Many high schools offer AP courses. AP courses range from English and math, to legal studies and foreign language. There are some advantages to taking AP courses they are as follows:

- Allows the student to get experience in college coursework.
- Are viewed as more rigorous courses than regular high school courses.
- College credit may be earned.
- Cost far less than regular college courses.

However, before you start taking AP courses, these items may affect your decision. They are as follows:

- Credits may not be accepted at all colleges.
- You must take the AP tests to obtain the college credits.
- A score of 4 and 5 are needed to transfer credits to many selective colleges.
- A score of 3 is a passing score.
- The tests are not free.

If possible, AP courses should be taken because these courses will prepare the student for college, even if the student does not take the AP examination. Remember, you want to obtain credit for college courses while in high school, or before you get to college, if you are an adult learner. Even if the course is academically challenging, it makes no sense if you take a hard course and not get college credit. Some schools, or school districts may cover the cost of the exams. I would recommend that you check with your student's school. Finally, you may take the AP exam without enrolling in an AP class. However, you are expected to know the material of the subject for which you are testing.

International Baccalaureate Program
https://www.ibo.org

The second way to earn college credit is by enrolling in the **International Baccalaureate Program, or IB**. An IB education provides opportunities to develop both disciplinary and interdisciplinary understanding that meet rigorous standards set by institutions of higher learning around the world. IB programs offer curriculum frameworks and courses that are broad and balanced, conceptual and connected (International Baccalaureate Organization, 2013, p.2).

IB is a smaller program than AP. However, they are very similar, with the exception that IB courses offer a more holistic, global approach to the subject than AP courses; furthermore, IB students can earn an IB diploma. High schoolers who have embraced IB's global educational philosophy can elect to earn an IB diploma, which is recognized by colleges around the world (Pannoni, 2014, p.1).

My advice for the IB program is similar to the AP program. If possible, IB courses should be taken because these courses will prepare the student for college.

CLEP TEST (College-Level Examination Program)
https://clep.collegeboard.org

What are CLEP exams?

Put simply, CLEP exams allow degree seekers with prior knowledge of introductory college topics the opportunity to take an exam demonstrating their mastery rather than taking the class itself. The overall purpose of CLEP exams is to reward existing knowledge and make it easier for students to earn college credit (Landry & McWhirter, 2018).

The advantages of CLEP are as follows:
- You do not have to take a class to test for CLEP.

- The fee is very low compared to regular college courses.
- There are numerous testing centers and sites.
- This process saves time.
- Active military members and immediate family can take the test without charge.
- Failures do not show up on your academic record.
- Passing several examinations may lessen you time in college.
- Adult learners can take the CLEP test.

Please be aware that:
- The test is not free and there is no refund if you do not pass.
- Not all colleges accept CLEP credit, please check with your College's Registrar.

Straighterline
https://www.straighterline.com/

If you are an adult learner, or if your high school does not offer AP, IB, or dual enrollment programs, or even if you simply do not qualify for those programs, Straighterline is for you. Straighterline happens to be one of my favorite college course programs because it allows high school students, and adult learners, the chance to take academically rigorous courses for a very low price.

Straighterline offers many general education courses, along with many introductory courses, starting at $59.00. There is a $99.00 monthly fee. These courses are approved and recognized by the American Council on Education. With your monthly fee, and the cost of the course, you will receive an e-Book, along with online tutoring, if needed. You have up to a year to complete the courses selected. Also, Straighterline will send your transcripts to your selected college, or employer, without a charge.

As a College Dean, my former University accepted Straighterline credits. When I had students with financial aid problems, I would recommend them to use Straighterline so they could get their grades up to get their financial aid back.

My niece used Straighterline. She had one math class standing between her and graduation. She failed the course. Because her private college was very expensive, she tried to take the course at the local community college. In order to do this, she would have had to register and pay for courses she did not need in order to earn the 3-credit hour math course. Her college was not on Straighterline's partner school list, but she called her school's registrar's office and they sent her an email to let her know they accepted Straighterline's credits. She took the math course and passed it. She then transferred the Straighterline credit back to her institution and received her degree. Straighterline is a valuable asset when trying to lower the costs of college and lessen the time spent in college.

These are some other advantages of Straighterline:
- Offers adult learners and high school students a chance to take college courses online.
- E-Books are included with the costs.
- Over 2,000 institutions accept Straighterline's college credits.
- Failure of a course in Straighterline, does not affect your academic standing.

- Courses cost drastically less than community college prices.
- Students have up to a year to complete course work.
- Taking courses will help determine if a student is ready for college or determine the right college fit.

Please be aware of the following:

- Certain business and science courses may cost more.
- Many of the science courses also have labs and lab kits are not included in the $59 or $99 monthly costs, but are additional costs.
- Please consult the university or college registrar of the school you may attend to confirm that Straighterline credits are accepted.
- Straighterline is not a college, but offers college courses that may be transferred to certain colleges and universities.

Dual Enrollment And Early College

Dual enrollment and early college are two options that many high schools offer students to ensure that high school students graduate and go on to college. Dual enrollment allows students to take college courses while attending high school. Early college allows students to take college courses that can be used for their high school requirements, as well as their college requirements. Many students graduate from high school with a diploma and an associate's degree from both programs. I would highly recommend this route over the others mentioned because this route is free.

However, for a school to offer these programs, it must be connected with a local community college. Please check to see if your high school offers these programs. Also, you can check your state's Department of Education webpage to get more information about dual enrollment and early college programs.

CHAPTER FOUR:

Accreditation

What is accreditation? According to the (Council for Higher Education Accreditation, 2015), "Accreditation" is the review of the quality of higher education institutions and programs. In the United States, accreditation is a major way that students, families, government officials, and the press know that an institution or program provides a quality education.

Whether a college, university, or program is accredited is vitally important:

- Students who want federal (and sometimes state) grants and loans, need to attend a college, university, or program that is accredited.
- Employers ask if a college, university, or program is accredited before deciding to provide tuition assistance to current employees, evaluating the credentials of new employees, or making a charitable contribution.

- The federal government requires that a college, university, or program be accredited in order to be eligible for federal grants and loans or other federal funds.
- State governments require that a college, university, or program be accredited when they make state funds available to students or institutions and when they allow students to sit for state licensure examinations in some professional fields (Council for Higher Education Accreditation, 2015).

Accreditation can be extremely confusing; however, not being aware of its importance can cost you money, time, and loss of employment opportunities. Let me give you an example. In my role as an Academic Dean, I had to listen to three angry students. Why were they angry? Well, they attended a nationally accredited college in the area. They were told that the school was accredited, and they could receive financial aid. The students were convinced because the counselor showed them the accreditor and they were able to receive federal financial aid.

Feeling confident, the students enrolled in the college's criminal justice program. What the admissions officer failed to tell the students was that nationally accredited college courses are very hard to transfer to regionally accredited schools. The admissions officer failed to mention that our city's police department (San Antonio, Texas) does not accept degrees from nationally accredited colleges. The students were even more upset because this university was more expensive than the community college and the state university in town. I empathized with the students. However, because my university was one of a few that accepted nationally accredited credits, the students were able to transfer to my university and graduate with a regionally accredited degree that was recognized by the San Antonio Police Department.

I hope this story has piqued your interest in accreditation. Students, parents, and adult learners need to be well-versed in accreditation. In this chapter, I am going to give you the down-and-dirty-quick version of accreditation. Hopefully, this information should be enough to keep you out of degree-mills and help you choose the right college.

There are two major college accreditation names to know at this point: regional and national accreditation. In my opinion, regional accreditation is the "gold standard" of accreditation. Colleges and universities, non-profit and for-profit, such as Yale, Harvard, Howard, Strayer, Stanford, Florida State, Ohio State, UCLA, Walden, Emory, and countless community colleges are primarily regionally accredited colleges. Even though some people may think that nationally accredited schools are the gold standard because the word "nationally" sounds like it has greater reach and is more encompassing, this is not the case.

A student and an adult learner should be more concerned about which regional accreditor, accredits the college or university. There are six, and only six, regional accreditation agencies for colleges and universities. They are as follows:

- **Middle States Association of Colleges and Schools**
  - o **States:** New York, Pennsylvania, Delaware, Maryland, and Washington D.C.
  - o **Sample colleges and universities:**

- New York University
- Morgan State University
- Howard University
- Penn State University
- University of Delaware
- Strayer University

https://www.chea.org/regional-accrediting-organizations#middle-states

- **New England Association of Schools and Colleges**
  - **States:** Maine, Massachusetts, Connecticut, Vermont, New Hampshire, and Rhode Island
  - **Sample colleges and universities:**
    - Yale University
    - Babson College
    - Bennington College
    - Brown University
    - Bowdoin College
    - Colby-Sawyer College

https://www.chea.org/regional-accrediting-organizations#new-england-institutions

- **North Central Association of Colleges and Schools (Now known as Higher Learning Commission)**
  - **States:** Missouri, Colorado, Illinois, Minnesota, Ohio, West Virginia, Michigan, Kansas, Iowa, Wisconsin, Indiana, Arizona, Arkansas, South Dakota, North

Dakota, Oklahoma, Nebraska, New Mexico, and
Wyoming

- o Sample colleges and universities:
    - New Mexico State University
    - Chicago State University
    - University of Chicago
    - Ohio State University
    - Kenyon College
    - National American University
    - University of Tulsa
    - Arkansas Baptist College

https://www.chea.org/regional-accrediting-organizations#north-central

- **Northwest Commission on Colleges and Universities**
    - o **States:** Montana, Alaska, Washington, Oregon, Idaho,
      and Nevada
    - o **Sample colleges and universities**
        - University of Alaska
        - Portland State University
        - Reed College
        - University of Nevada – Reno
        - University of Washington
        - Idaho State University
        - University of Providence

http://www.nwccu.org/

- **Southern Association of Colleges and Schools**

- o **States:** Georgia, Florida, Alabama, Texas, Virginia, South Carolina, North Carolina, Mississippi, Kentucky, Tennessee, and Louisiana
- o **Sample colleges and universities**
    - Florida State University
    - Stetson University
    - Emory University
    - Georgia State University
    - Spelman College
    - Texas Southern University
    - University of Alabama
    - Auburn University
    - University of Virginia
    - Norfolk State University
    - Sweet Briar College
    - Furman University
    - Rust College
    - Mississippi State University
    - University of Louisville
    - Northern Kentucky University
    - Duke University
    - Dillard University
    - Vanderbilt University

https://www.chea.org/regional-accrediting-organizations#southern

- **Western Association of Schools and Colleges**
    - o **States:** California and Hawaii
    - o **Sample colleges and universities**

- Chaminade University
- University of Hawaii – Manoa
- University of California – Berkley
- Pomona College
- Harvey Mudd College
- Loma Linda University
- University of Hawaii – Hilo

https://www.chea.org/regional-accrediting-organizations#western-senior

Remember, if you are planning to transfer to another regionally accredited college, you will have a better chance of transferring the credits if you are enrolled at a regionally accredited college or university. Regional accreditation is the "gold standard" of college and university accreditation for U.S. colleges and universities. Regional accreditation is the most widely recognized accreditation. Regionally accredited colleges and universities are accepted by most corporate tuition reimbursement plans. If you want to know if a school is regionally accredited, use the links below to help you.

https://www.chea.org/search-institutions
https://ope.ed.gov/dapip/#/home

What is national accreditation?

According to (Geteducated.com, 2018), the Council for Higher Education Accreditation (CHEA) also recognizes a number of "national accreditation agencies." These agencies are called "national agencies" because they aren't organized by and limited to regional geographic areas.

These national agencies have historically focused on approving career, vocational, and trade schools that offer certificates and degrees. Because of the specialized focus, the requirements to earn a certificate or degree from a nationally accredited school are not as standardized as a regionally accredited school. Nationally accredited schools are reviewed every 3-5 years to ensure that they still meet the requirements (GetEducated.com, 2018).

The two most popular "national" college accreditation agencies recognized by CHEA are:

Distance Education & Training Council (DETC)

Accrediting Commission of Career Schools and Colleges (ACCSC)

Other national accreditation agencies include:

Council on Occupational Education (COE)

Transnational Association of Christian Colleges and Schools,

Accreditation Commission (TRACS) (GetEducated.com, 2018)

In most cases, many beauty and barber colleges, along with technical and trade schools, are nationally accredited. The sole purpose for many of these institutions is to prepare students for jobs in the workforce. There are a few colleges and universities that are nationally accredited. However, there are many regionally accredited community colleges and technical colleges that offer the same, if not more, disciplines as the nationally accredited institutions. From my experiences with students who have transferred from nationally accredited institutions, I would strongly recommend that you select a regionally accredited college or university. Here are some reasons for my recommendation:

- The majority of employers accepted regionally accredited degree; however, this is not the case with many nationally accredited degrees.

- If you decided to further your education with a nationally accredited degree, your college choices might be limited to just nationally accredited schools, with very few options for obtaining a regionally accredited degree.

- Credit transfers from nationally accredited colleges to regionally accredited colleges are limited at best, but rejected for the most part.

- With very few exceptions, regionally accredited colleges and universities will not hire an instructor who graduated from a nationally accredited college or university.

When talking to a college admissions officer:

- **Always** ask if the school is **regionally** accredited. If the admissions officer tells you that the school is accredited, make sure he or she specify whether the college is a regionally or a nationally accredited school.

- Ask to see the college or university catalogue to confirm the institution's accreditation. Remember, if you do not see one of the regions mentioned in this chapter, then the college or university is **not** regionally accredited.

- Check the college's webpage to find out if it is regionally accredited. If you do not see one of the regions mentioned in this chapter, then the institution is **not** regionally accredited.

- An institution's eligibility for financial aid does not guarantee that the institution is regionally accredited. You have to confirm and verify that the institution is regionally accredited.
- If you are still not sure, check the Council of Higher Education Accreditation's webpage at: https://www.chea.org/search-institutions, or the United States Department of Education's webpage at: https://ope.ed.gov/dapip/#/home.

If I seem more partial to regionally accredited colleges over nationally accredited colleges, you are right! Why? The Accrediting Council for Independent Colleges and Schools, also known as ACICS, was once the largest national college accrediting agency in the United States. Recently, the United States Department of Education revoked ACICS status because of fraud, deceptive practices, low graduations rates, and lower gainful employment rates at many of its institutions. According to (Waldman, 2015), just 35 percent of students at a typical ACICS-accredited four-year college graduate, the lowest rate for any accreditor. Nationally, the graduation rate at four-year schools is around 59 percent.

According to (Bidwell, 2018), the Accrediting Council for Independent Colleges and Schools (ACICS) lost its federal recognition largely due to its oversight of the for-profit college chains, Corinthian Colleges and ITT Technical Institute, both of which closed their doors in recent years and have been the target of complaints from former students claiming the institutions defrauded them.

Another ACICS college, Florida Technical College, reached a $600,000 settlement with the Department of Justice earlier this year over allegations that the school received financial aid for ineligible students. The college allegedly submitted falsified high school diplomas for 27 students, resulting in more taxpayer money flowing to the school at the expense of students who took on debt. The school denied any wrongdoing in the settlement (Flores, 2018).

There have been a few developments since this ruling in 2016. Reggie B. Walton, a U.S. District Court judge for the District of Columbia, wrote in a 66-page opinion that the Education Department under President Barack Obama had "procedurally erred" in terminating the Accrediting Council for Independent Colleges and Schools, violating the Administrative Procedure Act. Walton remanded the case to Education Secretary Betsy DeVos to consider the relevant evidence. The opinion does not immediately undo the termination, but it paves the way for the Trump administration to potentially reverse the Obama-era decision (Harris 2018).

Remember, ACICS was the largest national accreditor in the United States. In my observation, most nationally accredited colleges lure low-income, first-generation college students, and adult learners, with a lack of knowledge about how the college process works, into their low-academic performing, high-cost, low yield and return, colleges. These colleges prey on the most vulnerable students by offering them a worthless degree that will not be accepted by most regional colleges. In addition to this, many of these students will be saddled with student loan debt. If the students even graduate, many will never obtain the high paying careers promised by an unethical admissions officer. Nor are they assisted with the placement for these high paying careers that were dangled like carrots to draw them into their doors in the first place!

I am not overly-ecstatic about many regionally accredited for-profit colleges either, but at least the students at these institutions have a chance to transfer to other colleges and achieve fairly decent careers. Also, if it were not for some of these colleges, many of the students attending the nationally accredited for-profit colleges would never have a chance to earn a regionally accredited degree.

Therefore, I cannot recommend any student or adult learner to attend a nationally accredited school. Many of these institutions have made fortunes off the ignorance of its students. Some are still making fortunes. Moreover, there are too many regionally accredited schools that offer the same majors as the nationally accredited institutions for much less. I know there are some "bad players" in the regionally accredited college world too, but they are scrutinized and closed if changes are not made promptly.

If a college or university staff lies about its accreditation (even by hiding details), then it will lie about its programs, its academic rigor, and its commitment to your success.

Programmatic Accreditation

What is programmatic accreditation? Programmatic accreditation can apply to programs, departments, or schools that are part of a larger college or university (law school, business school, etc.). The accredited school or program may be as large as a college or school within a university or as small as a curriculum within a discipline, or career field (GetEducated.com, 2018). Simply put, your area of study may, or may not, be programmatically accredited at your selected university. Depending on your area of study, this may be an area of concern.

Programmatic accreditation may be confusing if you are unaware of the academic and occupational requirements of your area of study. Students, or adult learners, must be aware of the professional organizations that provide endorsements for their area of study. First, a college or university can be regionally accredited; however, some of its programs may not have programmatic endorsements. This can cause major problems for engineering, allied health, education, and social work majors. The occupations for these majors require that college programs are recognized by the appropriate accrediting agencies. One the other hand, it may be a college or university's desire to be programmatically accredited in areas such as music, journalism, and dance, but for these majors, programmatic accreditation is not required to work in these fields.

However, if you plan to work in higher education, or attend a more selective graduate school, these areas of study may require programmatic accreditation. Once again, programmatic accreditation is specific to the student's area of study. Depending on the area of study, programmatic accreditation may, or may not be required.

The chart below is a small sample of disciplines that require programmatic accreditation and a small sample of those that do not require programmatic accreditation. Information about your area of study's accrediting agency is on this website: https://www.chea.org/programmatic-accrediting-organizations.

Please note, this chart is only an example, information from the accreditors may change at any time.

Programmatic Accreditation needed for undergrad studies	Yes	No
Area of Study		
Music		x
Allied Health/Nursing	x	
Engineering	x	
Journalism		x
Social Work	x	
Business	x	x
Education – Teaching	x	
English		x
Library Science	x	
Counseling	x	

C H A P T E R   F I V E :

Three Rules for Finding the Right College

According to the Washington Post, there are 5,300 colleges and universities in the United States (Selingo, 2015). If you are planning to apply for federal financial aid, you can only select one out of the 5,300 colleges. Which college is right for you? To find the right college, you must ask yourself a few basic questions:

- Do you want to leave your city or state to attend college?
- Do you want to attend a large university or small college?
- Do you want to attend a Historically Black College or University, gender specific college, military college, or religious school?
- Are you more comfortable in a small town or large city?

These are just a few questions that will help you narrow down your college search. In addition to asking these questions, I base my college advising from these three key questions.

- Does this college fit you academically?
- Does this college fit you socially?
- Does this college fit you financially?

In my experience, students drop out of college for one, or all, of these three reasons.

Does This College Fit You Academically?

Can you handle the work and the workload? Are your writing skills up to the challenge? All colleges should have academically-rigorous courses. You should feel challenged. However, some colleges are expecting even more. You need to know the college's expectations. You need to be honest with yourself, and ask yourself this question: can I handle the college's academic expectations? These are some questions you need to think about before enrolling at any college.

First, you have to make sure you can do the course work. As a former Academic Dean, if a student did not have college credits in English or Math, he or she would have to take the college's placement test. If the student did not pass the placement test, he or she would have to enroll in the college-preparatory courses, at full cost.

This is the reason why I recommend that students and adult learners use Straighterline.com. I would rather a student pay $59.00

to take a remedial class on Straighterline, than to the pay full price ($1,000 or more) at a regular college. Furthermore, the student could take the Algebra or English courses on Straighterline, and then transfer the credits to the college.

During the process of selecting colleges, be honest with yourself. If you know you were not a great student, and your G.P.A. was a 2.3, you may want to put Harvard or Yale on the backburner, go to your local community college, prove you can handle college courses, and then choose a more selective college or university.

If you are aware of some academic deficiencies you may have, select schools that have strong remedial programs, along with TRIO and student support programs. You may want to look at colleges with smaller class sizes, rather than a university with a lecture-style class of more than 50+ students.

Many students select colleges because relatives and friends are alumni. Please remember, just because your mom or dad attended a certain college, does not mean you have to attend that same college. Your folks may have been academically smarter than you, or you may be smarter than them. Make sure you are choosing a college for *your* needs.

Some colleges and universities cater to adult learners because they know many of these students have to juggle career and family. However, some universities are not flexible and are extremely rigid in their academic process. If family, career, and your social life are important to you, please think long and hard before enrolling at an academically-rigid university.

I was a Student Support Director in the Allied Health department of a college. I was talking with a student who enrolled in the nursing program because her mother was a graduate of the program. However, after a year in the program, she dropped out. She said that nursing became her life and she was always stressed out. She was not happy. She enrolled in the surgical technologist program and graduated a happy woman. Know where you stand academically and chose the right college that will meet you where you stand and take you further than you could ever imagine!

Does This College Fit You Socially?

After completing my Bachelor's degree, I had some major decisions to make about graduate school. I received numerous offers, but I decided to attend Pittsburg State University in Pittsburg, Kansas. This university was in the rural part of Southeastern Kansas. I selected this university because they offered me a full-tuition scholarship. Even though the university was a great financial fit, it was not a good social fit for me.

First, I was used to being in a large city with a variety of cultural events. Second, I was comfortable with having a variety of cultures on campus. Moreover, I was used to attending progressive churches that focused on social justice. In contrast, Pittsburg, Kansas was not a large city, not to mention, its Wal-Mart Supercenter was larger than the Pittsburg Mall. Hanging out at Sonic and ordering a cherry-lime aid, was usually the social event for most weekends for the community there.

While in Kansas, I felt like I was five years behind culturally compared to my peers on the east and west coasts. I felt that most churches in the city were extremely one-dimensional and not very progressive. I had three close friends while in Pittsburg, and I was depressed for most of the academic year. This depression affected my academic outlook, and I knew I had to transfer to a college that would fit my social needs.

I am sharing this story to prevent you from making the same mistakes I made. In my opinion, you may experience success even if you dislike the city your college is located; however, your chances of graduation are very slim when you dislike the college and the city where the college is located. Before you make a final selection concerning a college or university, make sure you like the college. You want to make sure the college will have a variety of cultural events that appeal to you during the academic year. If you value diversity, make sure you witness it at the university, and in the city as well. While you are touring the college, speak with a large sample of current students to get a "real" feel of the college.

As I mentioned in chapter one, I attended two undergraduate colleges before I found the college that was the fit right socially and academically. Had I put more effort into touring colleges and doing more research, I would have saved time and money. Eventually, Norfolk State University, (classified as a Historically Black College or University, or HBCU) was the right academic and social fit for me. The university was in historic Norfolk, Virginia. Numerous churches were progressive and embraced social justice. There was a rich black history, colonial history, military history, and indigenous history there. Also, Norfolk was a major college and military city, surrounded by a cluster of other large metropolitan cities. Therefore, concerts, art exhibits, and major festival were constantly taking place throughout the region year-round.

Even though I enjoyed the city of Miami, and the college I attended while residing there, I was not satisfied with the academic environment of the college. During my time there, the college lacked hybrid programs and dual majors. Socially, I made many friends, but because of the college's small student population at that time, I felt limited. Norfolk State University was an institution that was large enough to serve me, but small enough to know me. It was the perfect fit. I thrived at Norfolk State University because I loved the institution, and thoroughly enjoyed being in the Hampton Roads area.

I want to be very clear, not everything at Norfolk State University was perfect, but the university offered enough for me by way of activities and student support to keep me satisfied. Also, I want to add, I toured Norfolk State University before I decided to transfer there. I did not do this with the first college I selected.

In short, make sure you are completely satisfied with the college or university. If you enjoy the community that your college is located, then this should be integrated into your process for choosing the right college. All of these factors play an important part in retention and graduation. When you are happy with your college socially and academically, and love the community that the college is in, you are probably less likely to transfer to another institution, causing you to waste time and money.

Does This College Fit You Financially?

Does this college fit you financially? In an all honesty, I think this factor plays less of a role than the previously mentioned factors. Why? First, you can work while attending college to defray costs. Secondly, the college may provide work-study to assist you with your financial needs. Also, the college or university may have scholarships to cover the cost that your Pell Grant and other student aid may not cover. Finally, you can always apply for student and private loans. Ensure that student and private loans are your **last** resort, and only use what you absolutely need.

I want to be very clear, I am not saying that college finances are not important. If the college you want to attend is $48,000 a year, and your student aid only covers $10,000, but there is a second or a third choice that is much less in cost than your first choice, I am going to strongly advise you to consider the second or third choices. With that said, examine your college choices wisely. If you are majoring in English and a state institution's tuition is $14,000 a year, a private college's tuition is $20,000 a year, and both academic programs are nearly identical, I am going to advise you to select the state college. However, if the private college offers more financial assistance to cover the cost, and is less than the state college, then I will advise you to make your decision based on the social and academic aspects of the two institutions.

It is important to note that tuition is only one aspect of college costs. You must factor in room and board as well as other miscellaneous costs.

Let's look at the least expensive public and private institutions in the US for 2018-2019:

Brigham Young University – Provo, Utah

- **TUITION & FEES** $5,620 (2018-19) /*Non-L.D.S.* (Non Latter Day Saints)
- **ROOM AND BOARD** $7,628 (2018-19)
- **TOTAL ENROLLMENT** 34,334 (US News and Report, 2018)

Total: $13,248

Chadron State College – Chadron, Nebraska

- **TUITION & FEES** $4,290 (2018-19)/*Out-Of-State Tuition*
- **ROOM AND BOARD** $5,930 (2018-19)
- **TOTAL ENROLLMENT** 3,033 (US News and Report, 2018)

Total: $10,220

Looking at the two institutions' tuition, along with room and board, Chadron State College, by the numbers, seems like it is the apparent winner. However, we need to take a few things into consideration. First, and foremost, Brigham Young University is a far more nationally recognized university than its counterpart. Unless you are from Nebraska, how many people have ever heard of Chadron State College? Chadron State College could have excellent academic programs, but B.Y.U. has the name recognition employers will recognize, and in the long run, may be the better financial choice.

If you are an active member in good standing in the Latter-Day Saints community, it is a good chance the tuition at B.Y.U. will be reduced. Underrepresented minorities may benefit financially by attending B.Y.U. Why? Some universities may not be in regions where there is a great deal of diversity, and in some cases, universities will offer qualified minorities full- or partial scholarships to achieve a more diverse campus setting.

There is a three-thousand-dollar difference between the costs of the two institutions. Work-study, scholarship, or a family contribution could make up this difference. So, before selecting the college with the cheapest tuition, look at your long-term goals. Tuition may be less expensive at some institutions, but you may make $10,000 less because you did not choose the school with the better name recognition. To further investigate the real value of many institutions, look at the job placement and earnings of students who have graduated from these colleges. These statistics are is an important part of the financial fit as well.

We have to look at how the other aspects, social and academic, play a role in the financial aspect of college. If we look at these colleges with this limited scope, we are bound to still make the wrong selection. First, B.Y.U. is a very selective college. If you are not ready academically, you stand a slim chance of getting accepted into this university. Also, B.Y.U. is not a small institution. It has 34,000 students. So, if you like smaller colleges, Chadron State College, with 3,033 students, may be the right fit. B.Y.U. is affiliated with the Latter Day Saints Church and may require you to follow strict rules and guidelines. On the other hand, Chadron State College is non-sectarian (not religious), but it is in a rural town on the far northwest side of Nebraska. So, even if these two colleges are a financial fit, are they a social and academic fit for you?

In closing, select the college you are going to be academically and socially happy with, as long as the college is not drastically more in cost than your other choices selected. If the college is the right fit, you will find a way to make the financial piece work.

CHAPTER SIX:

Community College: What You Should Know

I attended Brevard Community College (Now Eastern Florida State College) in Cocoa, Florida. I was in the TRIO Program, a program for first-generation college students that provided moral support, academic support, and financial assistance. Brevard Community College provided my small community a chance to see college sports through its many sports teams, a chance to view plays and fine art exhibits, as well as to hear renowned guest lecturers during many of its cultural and academic events. Brevard Community College was truly a college for the Brevard County Community.

You may have a community college in your area that provides similar programs and events. However, **community and junior colleges serve two basic purposes: to prepare students to transfer to a four-year college, or to prepare students for the workforce.** In most cases, if students earn an Associates of Arts degree, they are, more than likely, planning to attend a four-year college. If students earn an Associates of Science degree, they are, more than likely, planning to enter the workforce. Most community colleges have a liberal arts track and a vocational/technical track.

The Great Depression marked a great boom in junior college enrollment. This period was caused primarily by young adults unable to find work coupled with significant increases in high school graduates. From 1929 to 1939, enrollment jumped from 56,000 to 150,000 (Brint & Karabel, 1989). With college education perceived since the 1920s as the avenue for social and economic upward mobility, social attitudes, too, played a major role in the expansion of the junior colleges. During this same period, the American Association of Junior Colleges membership was forming a consensus relative to the curriculum. The concept of a two-track curriculum was gaining momentum; transfer and terminal tracks would be established (Drury, 2003).

Students and adult learners, if finishing a four-year degree is your goal, then the transfer track is going to be the best option for you while attending a community college. There are some advantages to attending a community college. The prices are lower at community colleges compared to most four-year colleges and universities. Community colleges offer flexible schedules and night courses, not to mention much smaller courses. Community colleges offer a two-year degree. At most four-year colleges and universities, after two years, students earn credit hours and not a two-year degree. Community colleges also offer students the chance to improve their grades. If you did not do well in high school, the community college offers a chance to improve your Grade Point Average to transfer to a more selective college or university.

The disadvantages of community colleges are that they offer limited majors and curriculum. If you plan on majoring in a unique field, you may want to seek out a four-year college or university that offers the field that interests you. Community colleges keep lower cost because they offer basic majors. Since many community colleges do not have campus dorms, you may miss out on developing social bonds and experiencing the full college experience.

If you must have a two-year degree in hand, I will suggest that you attend a community college. If you are planning on entering the vocational/technical track, I would suggest enrolling at a community college. If grants and scholarship completely fund your community college education, or if your student aid covers most of your educational needs, I would recommend you enroll at your community college.

However, if you are a working adult or student that cannot attend a regular class due to work and family commitments, or if you have to pay tuition out of pocket, I would recommend Straighterline. Straighterline is competing with the community colleges for students needing general education courses. Also, Straighterline is less expensive than courses at most community colleges. Furthermore, your academic record is not affected if you fail a Straighterline course. Straighterline offers college courses that are recognized by the American Council on Education, but Straighterline is not a college. Once your course is completed with Straighterline, you transfer it to the college and get the academic credit. You will not receive a grade, just the academic credit. If you plan to use Straighterline, make sure your college is on the partnership list. If the college is not on the list, check with the college's registrar's office to insure they will take the college credits. Make sure to get the approval in writing from the registrar.

CHAPTER SEVEN:

For-Profit Colleges

I want to start this chapter by saying that all colleges and universities need a profit to operate. If a student has a debt with a for-profit, or not-for-profit institution, he or she will not receive a degree of completion, nor be able to order transcripts, or transfer credits to another institution of higher learning until the debt is paid. Organizations cannot run without funding; therefore, for-profit colleges, and not-for-profit colleges, have to make a profit. However, funding sources and consumer outcomes, in my view, separate for-profit colleges from not-for-profit colleges.

In the not-for profit education environment, funding comes from the federal government, endowments, donations from wealthy benefactors, foundations, and grants. In reality, many of these institutions are subsidized by the federal government. However, in the for-profit education environment, funding comes from corporations who have to answer to shareholders. The shareholders view education as a business and invest in education for a profit. Money is the bottom line for these education investors.

On the other hand, making a profit is important for not-for-profit institutions as well, but it answers to the federal government. Individuals, or corporations, who donate to these institutions usually receive a generous tax write-off from the federal government. Not-for-profits colleges and universities that receive money from corporations do not have the pressure to turn a profit because the government is going to give the corporations a tax write-off regardless of the university's performance. It's that simple. **Note:** a not-for-profit college or university can be government funded or privately funded.

In the first chapter, I mentioned "reputable" for-profit colleges. Having served in leadership at two for-profit universities has opened my eyes to the reality of for-profit education. Shareholder demand, corporate leadership, and academic leadership will determine if a for-profit institution will be reputable. Please be aware that corporations own most for-profit universities. If the corporation does not respect and follow the advice of its academic leadership, this could lead to a watered-down curriculum, lax admission policies and standards, and low retention and graduation rates. However, the academic leadership has to be aware that the institution has to make a profit because the shareholders demand it.

A reputable for-profit college usually will have educated shareholders that are aware of the process concerning higher education administration. At most reputable for-profit universities, the corporate division and the academic division will work together to come up with innovative programs and will use technology to spur profits. Reputable for-profits colleges seek out opportunities and programs that will bring revenue to the university, while benefiting the student population it serves.

For example, I worked for a for-profit university that had an open enrollment policy. This policy allowed any student with a high school diploma to be admitted to the college. Nevertheless, the student had to take a placement test to determine college readiness. If the student failed the placement test, he or she had to take prep English and math. The student had to pass both courses within two quarters.

If the student did not pass either course within two quarters, the student was dismissed. The institution did not want the student to be saddled with debt. This process allowed the student a chance to improve his or her skills, while being a part of the college experience. This also increased the universities enrollment. In most cases, students who were serious about their college careers, worked hard to pass the college-preparation courses.

On the other hand, I worked for an institution that did not have these safe guards and allow the student to repeat these courses numerous times. Unfortunately, when the student aid ended, if the student did not have another form of payment, he or she was dismissed. In many cases, less reputable for-profit colleges leave the student saddled with debt, no funds to attend another college, and no degree earned.

In the past, many not-for-profit colleges and universities did not view online/brick-and-mortar for-profit colleges very favorably. However, for-profit colleges' revenue and interest by non-traditional students did not go unnoticed by not-for-profit colleges. Now, the not-for-profit colleges are using the same model as the once despised for-profit-colleges to increase enrollment and profits. Because of this, many for-profit colleges and universities will either have to merge, offer specialized degree programs, or close. The competition is fierce.

In my expert opinion, as a former academic dean for a for-profit university, I would not recommend a high school student to enroll at one of these institutions. My view is that adult learners who do not have flexible schedules to attend a regular brick-and-mortar college should use for-profit universities as one of their options. With many of the not-for-profit colleges offering similar programs, unless the not-for-profit university is more expensive, or lacks an open admission policy, if you desire this, I would recommend that you consider a not-for-profit college. However, if you desire to attend a regionally accredited for-profit college or university, here are a few tips:

- The regionally accredited for-profit college or university usually should cost more than your state university, but less than your private not-for-profit college. In my view, if a for-profit college is more, or the same price, as your private not-for-profit college, I feel you may be paying too much.

- If the for-profit university has a bad reputation in the community, more than likely, it has a bad reputation in the business community as well. Think twice before enrolling.

- Read other peoples' reviews about the college. This may help you in your decision-making process.

- Look at the for-profit college or university's programmatic accreditation. In my view, when a for-profit has gone through the time to get extra accreditation, it is a plus for its students.

- Do not feel pressured to enroll. The admission counselors at most for-profit college will do almost anything to get you to enroll.

- If the buildings where the university is located is dirty and unkempt, you can usually expect the same quality in its education.

- Compare the curriculum to other for-profit and not-for-profit colleges. If it is lacking, you may not receive the education you are hoping for. Find another program that is on-par with other reputable colleges and universities.

- If you do enroll, pay close attention to the academic calendar. The academic calendar will provide deadlines for drops and adds, alone with withdrawals. Knowing this ahead of time will save you money if for any reason you have to withdraw from the program.

- Get it in writing. If you are offered a scholarship, or reduced tuition, make sure you get the promise in writing with official signatures.

- Remember, for-profit colleges are about the profit. You are the key to their profit. If you go in knowing this, you will be fine.

- Most for-profits are publicly traded companies. Look at the financial health of the company. You do not want to attend a college that is in danger of closing.

If you want to know more detailed information about for-profit colleges, I will provide a link so that you can look up your school. Former Senator, Tom Harkins, provided a report detailing the overall performance of for-profit colleges. This will further empower you to make a wise decision.

https://www.help.senate.gov/imo/media/for_profit_report/Contents.pdf

CHAPTER EIGHT

Things First-Generation and Adult Learners Need to be Aware of

- **College Prep Courses:**
  - College prep courses are not college courses. These courses are to prepare students for college courses. Usually, a student has to enroll in these courses when he or she did not pass the college placement test. Unfortunately, at most colleges, a student will still pay full tuition for these courses, but not earn any college credit. Many students take these courses; unfortunately, most run out of financial aid because of these courses. College prep courses are usually numbered from 060 – 099. Also, they use titles like: **intro to, elementary, or fundamentals of.** If you know you are deficient in math or English, you should take remedial courses before you get to college. In some states, you can opt out of taking these

courses, but I do not recommend this if you are struggling with math or English. I just do not recommend you take these courses at the college.

These are my recommendations:

- Take Straighterline prep courses ($59.00).
- Take Straighterline college English and math Courses ($59.00-$100.00).
- Study and take the CLEP English and math tests.
- If you are a high school student, take AP or IB courses and take the exam.
- If you are in high school, get into the Dual enrollment or early college program.

Straighterline is out-of-pocket, but you will still come out better financially by taking Straighterline courses. If you fail a Straighterline course, it does not show up on your academic record. Only if you pass the course will you receive a T (transfer) that will serve as a credit at your college or university. Please get a written email or letter from the college registrar's office if they are not on Straighterline's partnership list. If you take the CLEP English and math test, there is a certain score you must meet or exceed. The CLEP costs between $90.00- $100.00 and is non-refundable. Also, you have to make your own arrangements to study for the exam.

- **Electives and how to use them**

In college you have your general education courses: English, math, social sciences, and natural sciences; Core courses: your major courses; and electives: courses of interest and your choosing. Because electives are courses of interests that you can choose, most students chose easy courses that are not related to their majors. Doing this is a mistake. Use your elective courses as a minor. For example, if you are majoring in marketing, but want to venture in the entertainment and music industry, then use your elective credits to take courses such as, the business of music and music history. In some universities, five or more courses in an area can serve as a minor.

- **Military Students/ College or GI Bill**
  - Active and retired military students have to be extremely careful when selecting a college. Military students are prized because colleges and universities know the government will pay the student's tuition. Also, be wary of colleges that are overly eager to enroll active or retired military students. If you feel pressured or rushed, more than likely, the admissions officer has a quota to meet. It is wise to take all the information, such as the college catalogs and brochures, to a military educational advisor. Just because a college or university states that it is military friendly, does not mean it has your interest-at-heart.
  - All of the information in this book would also be beneficial to children of our active/affiliated military. However, if you are an active military student, if you attend a regional not-for-profit, or for-profit college, make sure they have an online degree program. Many military students are stationed

in various places during their military career. If a college does not have a flexible academic policy for active military students, or an online component, students could be wasting valuable GI benefits by having to withdraw from college when they receive orders for a new duty station.

o If the institution has a bad reputation, you may not want to enroll.

o Military friendly colleges and universities have a veteran's affairs departments, or at a minimum, a veteran's admissions officer. Make sure this person has a college degree and has served in the military or has been a part of the military process.

o If you plan to further your education in the future, please attend a regionally accredited college or university. Some jobs require that your college or university is regionally accredited.

o If you are a high school student enrolled in ROTC, consider going into a college ROTC program. Many times, the military will pay for your four years of college, with an agreement that you serve four years in the military. If you are successful in most college ROTC programs, you may start your military career as an officer.

o It is important that active or retired military students get their Joint Service Transcripts. This step could save you some money and reduce your time in college.

• **Specialized training colleges/Culinary – Nursing – Seminary – Psychology**

o Colleges and universities have numerous majors and programs to choose from; however, there are institutions of higher learning that focus on specific subjects. For example, The Culinary Institute of America main focus is on food preparation and the business aspect of restaurant management. You would not attend this institution if you wanted to become an actor. Another example of a specialized institution of higher learning is seminaries. United Theological Seminary trains and teaches men and women who desire to work in the area of ministry. The programs at United Theological Seminary focus on items related to ministry and spirituality. You would not attend this institution for a degree in civil engineering.

o   If you attend a specialized school, make sure it is regionally accredited and programmatically accredited. For example, The Culinary Institute of America is accredited by The Middle States Commission on Higher Education https://www.ciachef.edu/accreditation/.

o   United Theological Seminary is accredited by The Higher Learning Commission (formerly known as: North Central Association of Colleges and Schools) and programmatically accredited by The Commission on Accrediting of the Association of Theological Schools http://united.edu/accreditation-association/.

o   There are many nationally accredited specialized schools and colleges. I do not recommend them because they are usually more expensive than the regionally accredited schools, and nationally accredited colleges credits rarely transfer to regionally accredited schools.

o Please remember that most colleges and universities offer programs that regionally accredited specialize schools offer. Many times, the college and universities programs are much lower in cost. Please compare programs and prices.

- **Transfer Credits**
  o When taking courses to transfer to another college or university, it is wise to take general education courses and introductory level courses such as: Introduction to Business, Introduction to Finance, Introduction to Marketing, and Introduction to Accounting. These are a few courses that usually transfer to other colleges and universities.
  o The higher the course level, the less likely you will be able to transfer the credit to another college or a university. For example, an Introduction to Business class, BUS 101, will have a better chance of transferring than a BUS 475 class.
  o If you are attending a community college, I recommend that you obtain an Associate of Arts degree before transferring. Colleges usually will accept the whole degree. However, if you transfer credits, they may not take all of them.
  o The more credits you transfer to other colleges, the more credits you will lose. This reason is why it is important to find the right college or university.
  o In some fields, such as nursing, your general education courses may transfer, but all of your core courses will have to be taken at the university you select, even if you are in your final year. Also, science courses usually have to be retaken if they are over five years, or older, on your college transcripts.

o The earlier your transfer, the fewer credits you lose.

o If you plan to transfer to another college, please review the other college's transfer policy.

- **Financial Aid**

  o The more courses you take before college (CLEP, AP, IB, and Straighterline) will save you money in the long run. If you are an adult learner, you may have to pay out-of-pocket for CLEP or Straighterline, but it is far more inexpensive than the most affordable community colleges. Pay now or pay later.

  o Admissions officers and financial aid officers are not your friends. These individuals are the employees of the colleges and universities they serve. They work in the interest of the college. Remember, education is not a business, but the process around it is. Do not be fooled. Knowledge is power.

  o Make sure you have an honest assessment of what you can contribute towards your education.

  o Student loans should be your last resort in obtaining your education. If you must use student loans, take only what you need. Remember, you will have to pay that money back.

  o Merit Scholarships are based on academic achievement. Need-based aid is income driven.

  o Make sure you ask about college work study, TRIO programs for first-generation college students, program specific scholarships, and athletic scholarship.

  o Make sure you fill out the FAFSA application correctly. If you are not sure about something, ask the financial aid officer. It is critical that you fill out the application correctly.

- o Know the deadlines for drop and add, last day to withdraw without financial penalty, and the last day to withdraw without academic penalty. I cannot say this enough, know the deadlines! Missing a deadline by one day could be the difference in paying $120.00 to pay $1,200.00. Most colleges will not remind you of these important dates.

- o Employment tuition reimbursement may be available if you are a working adult. Speak with your HR benefits representative concerning college tuition benefits. I earned two degrees with the help of my two companies' tuition reimbursement programs.

- o Remember, a generous financial aid package is not important if you dislike the college. Make sure the college is the right fit for you academically and socially.

- **Go to a school that has your major**

  - o Do not enroll at a college or a university that does not have the program you are desiring. If you want to enroll in a music program, I would not recommend that you select Florida Institute of Technology. F.I.T is a great school if you are looking to pursue a career in engineering, but glancing over their webpage, it would not be a wise choice for a student looking to major in voice performance to enroll there.

  - o If you desire a degree in television journalism, I would not recommend you attend a college with a general communication program. Mass communication and communication are two different programs.

- o I made the mistake of going to a college that offered the programs I desired; however, the university did not allow double-majors, nor did it have hybrid programs. Therefore, I had to transfer to a school that had a hybrid program. Had I done my homework, and asked the right questions, I would not have had to waste time or money at the first college. I am sharing my experience so that you will not make the same mistake I made.

- **Sitting out:**
  - o Remember, even taking a break could cost you more and delay your graduation progress. Many colleges and universities change their curriculum every three years. During this time, new courses can be added or modified. If you leave and sit out for two or more semesters or quarters, the university could have added new courses. For you to complete your degree, you may have to take addition courses. The university does this to ensure its students stay in school and complete the degree. In addition to this, it is a great money maker for the university. My advice to you is to stay in school. If you must take a break, make sure it is not more than one semester.

CHAPTER NINE:

Academic Currency

At present, the most widely accepted version of academic currency is the student credit hour (Johnstone, Ewell, and Paulson, 2010). Awarding a student a degree essentially involves ensuring that he or she has satisfactorily completed a series of required and elected courses that amount to fixed periods on task, accounted for regarding a given number of credit hours (Johnstone, Ewell, and Paulson, 2010). To ensure the quality of the degree, faculty from the awarding institution work together to be sure the topics for each of these courses fit into a coherent framework that leads to the learning objective that the institution has established for its graduates (Johnstone, Ewell, and Paulson, 2010). Finally, a regional accreditor is charged with publicly certifying that all this has taken place (Johnston, Ewell, and Paulson, 2010).

In short, every time a student passes a class, it earns him or her academic currency. The higher the grade in the course, the more points the student obtains. Also, following a process and schedule are key components in earning a degree which indicates that all credit hours have been obtained. As mentioned earlier in this book, regional, not national, accreditation is the preferred accreditation standard. This is according to the American Council on Education.

Terms:

1. **Cumulative G.P.A.:** Your cumulative GPA is your grade point average for all attempted courses in the program.
2. **Term G.P.A.:** Your Grade Point Average for that one term or semester.
3. **Credit Hours:** The number of hours assigned to a course (listed in both the online schedule of courses and the catalog)
4. **Quality Points:** The numerical value assigned to a grade.
5. **Earned Hours:** Credit hours for courses completed at college or university in which you earn a grade of D or higher. This total will also include any credit hours earned for transfer credits and test credits, though neither type of credit will factor into your GPA.
6. **Attempted Hours:** Credit hours for courses in which you earn a grade.
7. **Repeat/Credit:** This repeat option indicates that all grades received for all attempts of a course will be used when calculating the GPA.
8. **Repeat/Forgiveness:** This repeat option indicates that the grade received for the second attempt of a course will replace the grade earned for the first attempt in the GPA calculation.

Grades	Quality Points	Multiply	Credits earned	Equal	Points
A =	4	x	3.00	=	12
B =	3	x	3.00	=	9
C =	2	x	3.00	=	6
D =	1	x	3.00	=	3
F= *(no credit given for F or WF grades)*	0	x	0.00	=	0
					30 points

$$\frac{\text{Total Points Earned}}{\text{Total Credits Attempted}} = \text{Grade Point Average}$$

You would add all total points and credits attempted for each semester to obtain your cumulative G.P.A.

How to calculate the 67% completion rate. What is the 67% completion rate?

Example:

Credit Hours Earned (27) divided by Credit Hours Attempted (30) = Completion rate (90%) *(good standing)*

A 67 percent or above completion rate of your passed and attempted hours is need in order to continue receiving financial aid.

Examples of the term and cumulative G.P.A.s, completion rates for financial aid, and point values and grade points.

Which student has the best academic currency?

Student A/ Semester 1	Grade	Point Value	Credit Hours Earned	Credit Hour Attempted	Grade Points	Term GPA
English 101	A	4---->X	3.00	3.00	=12	
Math 101	B	3---->X	3.00	3.00	=9	
History 101	C	2---->X	3.00	3.00	=6	
Biology 102	C	2---->X	3.00	3.00	=6	
Speech 101	B	3---->X	3.00	3.00	=9	
			15	15	42/15	=2.8
Student A/ Semester 2						
English 102	A	4	3.00	3.00	12	
Math 102	A	4	3.00	3.00	12	
Physical Science	B	3	3.00	3.00	9	
World Religion	A	4	3.00	3.00	12	
			12	12	45/12	=3.75
			27	27		Cumulative GPA
				27	87/27	=3.22
			Financial aid 67%	100% good standing		

Credit Hours Attempted = 30

A 67 percent or above completion rate of your passed and attempted hours is need in order to continue receiving financial aid.

Examples of the term and cumulative G.P.A.s, completion rates for financial aid, and point values and grade points.

Which student has the best academic currency?

Student B/Semester 1	Grade	Point Value	Credit Hours Earned	Credit Hour Attempted	Grade Points	Term GPA
English 101	C	2----->X	3.00	3.00	=6	
Math 101	C	2----->X	3.00	3.00	=6	
History 101	C	2----->X	3.00	3.00	=6	
Biology 102	C	2----->X	3.00	3.00	=6	
Speech 101	B	3----->X	3.00	3.00	=9	
			15	15	33/15	=2.2
Student B/Semester 2						
English 102	B	3	3.00	3.00	9	
Math 102	B	3	3.00	3.00	9	
Physical Science	D	1	3.00	3.00	3	
World Religion	A	4	3.00	3.00	12	
			12	12	33/12	=2.75
			27	27		Cumulative GPA
				27	66/27	=2.44
			Financial aid 67%	100% good standing		

Credit Hours Attempted = 30

A 67 percent or above completion rate of your passed and attempted hours is need in order to continue receiving financial aid.

Examples of the term and cumulative G.P.A.s, completion rates for financial aid, and point values and grade points.

Which student has the best academic currency?

Student C/Semester 1	Grade	Point Value	Credit Hours Earned	Credit Hour Attempted	Grade Points	Term GPA
English 101	F	0----->X	0.00	3.00	=0	
Math 101	C	2----->X	3.00	3.00	=6	
History 101	D	1----->X	3.00	3.00	=3	
Biology 102	C	2----->X	3.00	3.00	=6	
Speech 101	D	1----->X	3.00	3.00	=3	
			12	15	18/15	=1.2
Student C/Semester 2						
BUS 101	C	2	3.00	3.00	6	
Math 102	C	2	3.00	3.00	6	
Physical Science	D	1	3.00	3.00	3	
World Religion	F	0	0.00	3.00	0	
			9	12	15/12	=1.25
			21	27		Cumulative GPA
			27		33/27	=1.22
			Financial aid 67%	77% good standing		

If you selected student A, you are correct. Why does student A have better academic currency than student B and C? What are some differences?

- Student A passed courses with higher grades; therefore, student A earned higher grade points. Higher grade points will lead to a higher-Grade Point Average.

- Student A and B both have a higher completion rate percentage than student C.

- The lower your completion rate, the greater the chance you will fall below the 67% completion guideline. Student C is at 77% compared to students A and B with 100% completion rate.

- Failing courses diminishes your academic currency and places you in jeopardy of losing financial aid assistance.

- Student C has a cumulative Grade Point Average under a 2.0 which places him on probation and may jeopardize his financial aid.

Financial Aid and Completion

To remain eligible for financial aid, students must progress toward completing their academic programs. Financial Aid Satisfactory Academic Progress (SAP) is checked at the time your FAFSA results are received and at the end of each academic term. All coursework, including repeated coursework, withdrawn courses and remedial coursework, is included in the SAP calculation. SAP standards are reviewed and have to be met each term:

1. A minimum cumulative grade point average of 2.0 or above; AND

2. A 67 percent or above completion rate of your passed and attempted hours. Your completion rate is calculated by dividing the number of basic education and undergraduate cumulative passed hours by the number of cumulative hours attempted; AND

3. Attempted credits for your first financial aid eligible program show that you can complete that program within the maximum timeframe (150 percent) of that program's length or your attempted credits for an additional financial aid eligible program show that you can complete that program within the maximum timeframe (100 percent) of that program's length; AND

4. Pass at least one attempted course within your most recent term of enrollment with a grade of "'D" or better (Aims Community College, 2018).

Outlined below is a description of each possible SAP status and action for resolution.

- **Good** - You have met all academic progress criteria required to be eligible for financial aid.
- **Warning** - Your cumulative GPA has fallen below 2.0 or your overall successful course completion rate has fallen below 67 percent or both. Because your previous term GPA and course completion rate were at or above the minimum levels, you have one remaining term in which to receive aid without any additional action on your part. However, your GPA and completion rate must be back to the minimum standards at the end of the next term in which you receive financial aid for you to maintain continued eligibility.
- **Ineligible** - You have had either a GPA below 2.0 or a course completion rate below 67 percent or both for two or more subsequent terms in which you have received financial aid.

You are **not** eligible for further financial aid at this time. If you feel there were extenuating circumstances that contributed to your situation, you may file an appeal requesting a reconsideration of your eligibility. If you wish to file an appeal you may contact the Financial Aid office.

- **Fail/Withdrawal** - You did not complete any of your courses for the last term you were enrolled. You are **not** eligible for further financial aid at this time. If you feel there were extenuating circumstances that contributed to your situation you may file an appeal requesting a reconsideration of your eligibility. If you wish to file an appeal, you may contact the Financial Aid office.

- **Maximum Timeframe** - You have attempted more than 150 percent of the credits required to complete your currently enrolled program. You are **not** eligible for further financial aid at this time. If you are pursuing a subsequent program at Aims, or if you feel there are extenuating circumstances that contributed to your situation, you may file an appeal requesting a reconsideration of your eligibility. If you wish to file an appeal, you may contact the Financial Aid office.

- **Probation** - The appeal of your academic progress status has been approved. You have been given **ONE** extra term in which to receive aid and meet the minimum eligibility criteria of a 2.0 or greater overall GPA and 67 percent or better overall course completion rate.

- **Academic Plan** - The appeal of your academic progress status has been approved. You are subject to the conditions outlined in your academic plan. As long as you maintain the conditions outlined in your plan, you are eligible to receive financial aid.

- **Review** - Financial Aid staff members are currently conducting a review of your academic progress status. A final determination on your status will be posted shortly. Should you have any questions or concerns, you may contact the Financial Aid office (Aims Community College, 2018).

Building strong academic currency is a sure way to avoid the pitfalls of not being eligible for financial aid. As you can see, course completion is critical, not only for your academic health, but your financial health as well. This is why I strongly advise students to take college courses, or CLEP testing, before they even get to college. Once again, the more college credits you have, the more academic currency you possess.

CHAPTER TEN:

Good Academic Advising: How It Can Help with Retention and Graduation

Academic advising is critical in the area of student persistence and graduation. An academic advisor sets the atmosphere and the expectations for the student. The academic advisor also informs the student of what is available at the college or university to ensure the student's persistence and graduation. I am going to give you a run-down of what I cover in my sessions when counseling a student. I think this will be extremely helpful so that you will know what to expect in your first counseling session, or at least what questions you should ask during these sessions. Once again, knowledge is power.

I usually start the counseling session by reviewing the college placement scores with the student. However, since I have been very adamant about using Straighterline and CLEP testing to obtain college credit, I am going to assume you have college credits, at least in English and math. Taking into account that you will not need college prep courses, I will start this advising process by reviewing transcripts and reviewing the program plan and concentration.

- **Review transcripts:**
  - At this time, I will communicate with the student about which courses may or may not transfer into the college or university. I make the student fully aware that the final decision concerning the student's transfer credits will come from the Registrar's Office.

- **Review the selected program plan/concentration:**
  - During this period, I will ask the student what his or her planned major will be, along with his or her concentration. For example, if a student is majoring in business (major), I will ask if he or she is going to focus on marketing, accounting, finance, economics, or organizational leadership (concentration).
  - If you have taken your general education courses before enrolling at your selected college, it will be important to know you major and concentration. Because of the academic currency you have earned through transfer credits, you will not have to take many general education courses. This will put you at your core and major core courses.
  - During this time, I will ask a series of questions focusing on your process for selecting your major and concentration.

o I will review any program prerequisite courses that must be taken.

o Review any changes to the selected program, if the student is re-enrolling at the same college.

o Review any requirement differences – If a student takes a break from college, new requirements could emerge during the student's break. This could cause the student to have to take more courses. So, instead of taking 15 courses, if you take a break and re-enroll, you may have 18 courses because of requirement changes.

o Review any course age. If the course was taken ten years ago, the student might have to repeat that course.

- **Discuss the recommended course sequencing:**

    o At this point, I would make recommendations of which courses the student should take for each semester.

    o I usually recommend that the student take less-challenging courses at the beginning of his or her academic career. I then advise the student to take more challenging courses in the mid-point of his or her career, coupled with less challenging courses. By doing this, the student will raise his or her G.P.A. If the student makes lower grades from the challenging courses in the mid-point of his or her academic career, they will at least have some higher grades in the less challenging courses taken, along with the more rigorous ones. Also, the higher G.P.A. at the beginning of the student's academic career will be a buffer from lower mid-point grades.

o Afterwards, I recommend the students to take the courses of their interests and less challenging courses at the end-point of his or her academic career to bring his or her grades up from the mid-point of his or her academic career, if needed.

- **Explain how students can accelerate through the program:**
  o CLEP Testing
  o Straighterline

- **Review/discuss the student support services available:**
  o Grammerly.com
  o College tutoring and resource center
  o Tutor.com
  o Khan Academy (YouTube)
  o Crash Course (YouTube)
  o University counseling services
  o Study groups

- **Academic Expectations:**
  o Attendance policy
  o An undergraduate G.P.A. of 2.0 must be maintained.
  o On-line and on-ground class expectations.
  o Time management for hours per week study and preparation.
  o Stress the importance of reviewing the university's academic calendar.

- Discuss Support Systems:
  - o Ask students if family, friends, or co-workers are aware of the decision to attend college?
  - o Ask if family and friends are supportive of the decision?
  - o Know the student's back ground to discussion any challenges that may arise.
  - o If the student is a first-generation college student, explain some of the challenges he or she may have.

- Set up an appointment for the new semester:
  - o Time, Date, and Location.

CHAPTER ELEVEN:

Words of Wisdom

As I started to write this chapter, two local colleges abruptly announced that they would be closing. The two colleges were nationally accredited Virginia College and Brightwood College. Education Corporation of America owns these two colleges. ECA also owns the Ecotech Institute, Golf Academy of America, and Culinard, which is the culinary arm of Virginia College. All of these colleges closed abruptly.

Why? The shutdown came after the college's accreditor (Accrediting Council of Independent Colleges and Schools) — itself a troubled organization that the United States Education Department had accused of oversight failures — notified the company that it would no longer endorse its programs. This shutdown caused potential investors to walk away from the financially struggling chain, according to a letter that Stu Reed, the company's chief executive, sent to students on Wednesday (Cowley, 2018).

According to the New York Times, almost 20,000 students will be affected by this untimely shut-down (Cowley, 2018). I had a chance to watch countless news outlets report on this tragic situation. I just shook my head once again in unbelief when I watched students upset because they were notified the colleges ECA owned were closing. Some students went to lunch and came back to a locked school. Many students were supposed to graduate and only had one day of classes left. However, now they will not get a chance to walk the aisle for graduation. I was most disgusted when a future student, just minutes before the college closed, paid his tuition in full, only to find out that the college closed **20 minutes later.** The student was convinced that the financial aid officer knew the school was closing. In this case, I side with the student.

Many students called other colleges to find out if their college credits would transfer, to their dismay, many of the colleges would not accept their college credits. Many students said they would turn to the government to get the loans written off. Even if the students are successful in this effort, they have lost time, and many will have to start the academic process all over again. In addition to this, the tax payers will have to foot this enormous bill while the parent corporation gets off with a slap-on-the-wrist, if that.

With that said, even if the Accrediting Council of Independent Colleges and Schools were to be reinstated by the Education Secretary, Betsy Devos, I would not recommend any students to attend these institutions. As I have said earlier, these colleges prey on the most vulnerable students. I strongly feel that the damage has been done to this accrediting agency. Its reputation speaks for itself.

Please be aware that not-for-profit private colleges also struggle as well. Even though many are regionally accredited, a few private liberal arts colleges have closed their doors too. In contrast to the private for-profit colleges, many regional not-for-profit colleges give students enough time to transfer to other colleges. Furthermore, most college credits obtained from these institutions transfer. Sadly, any college closure deeply impacts a student. There is a tool to find out the financial health of not-for-profit private colleges. It is called GuideStar: https://www.guidestar.org/Home.aspx. GuideStar allows the public to see a private not-for-profit institution's tax forms and fillings. It also allows the public to view salaries of the top staff of a not-for-profit college.

CHAPTER TWELVE:

What's Missing from this Book?

I purposely did not put two things in this book: How to fill out a college application and how to prepare for a college interview. All college applications and interviews are not the same. They vary greatly. I hope that you will start to review college applications very early. If you are interested in certain colleges, you need to start requesting information in the latter portion of your 10th-grade year, if you are a high school student. If you have read and followed the instructions in this book, you should be prepared for any college application because you would have done your research and prepared.

I did not place great emphasis on the college interview because I would prefer to meet students face-to-face or recommend a college advisor. However, I will provide a few resources in this chapter. I think this college blog is a great way to prepare for a college interview. The bloggers ask questions that the college interviewer may ask and then the blogger explains the reasoning behind the question. You may find this blog at: <u>https://blog.prepscholar.com/college-interview-questions-you-should-prepare-for</u>. I have also provided a website for those students that may need some help in the college application process. You can find this at: https://www.usnews.com/ education/best-colleges/articles/college-application-process. Finally, I found an excellent checklist from the College Board that I will post in this publication. I think this will be very useful to students needing guidance in this process.

COLLEGE APPLICATION CHECKLIST

Use this checklist to help you stay on top of your application tasks, paperwork and deadlines.

	College 1	College 2	College 3
Application deadlines			
Regular application deadline			
Early application deadline			
Grades			
Request high school transcript sent			
Request midyear grade reports sent			
Test Scores			
Send test scores (e.g., SAT)			
Send SAT Subject Test scores			
Send AP* scores			

Letters of Recommendation			
Number required			
Request recommendations			
Send thank-you notes			
Essays			
Number required			
Proof essay(s) for spelling and grammar			
Have two people read the essay(s)			
Final copy in application			
Interviews			
Interview date			
Send thank-you note(s) to the interviewer(s)			

Handout 4A page 1 of 2 College Counseling Sourcebook, 7th edition.

COLLEGE APPLICATION CHECKLIST (PAGE 2)

	College 1	College 2	College 3
Send and Track Your Application			
Save/copy all application materials			
Include application fee			
Sign application			
Confirm receipt of application materials			
Send supplemental material, if needed			
Give a copy to the school counselor			
Financial Aid Forms			
Priority financial aid deadline			
Regular financial aid deadline			
Submit FAFSA			
Submit CSS/Financial Aid PROFILE*, if needed			
Submit institutional aid form, if needed			
Submit state aid form, if needed			

After You Send Your Application			
Receive admission letter			
Receive financial aid award letter			
Accept financial aid package			
Housing forms completed and returned			
Send deposit			
Notify other colleges that you will not attend			

Source: Get it Together for College, 2nd ed. (College Board, 2011)

CHAPTER THIRTEEN:

The Do's and Don'ts of Applying to College

As I mentioned earlier, this book is to help you navigate through the college process. This book does not get into testing strategies, interview techniques, and essay writing skills. However, if this publication is used properly, it will save you a great deal of time and headache when it comes to finding the right college at the right price. I cannot emphasis this enough: Right social fit, right academic fit, and right financial fit equal admissions, retention, and graduation. Also, not all colleges are meant for all people. Find a regionally accredited college that is right for you. If you need my assistance for consultation, please email me at dr.jameswilcox@yahoo.com. I will be more than happy to share rates and services with you. You may also request me for speaking engagements at this email as well. Now to discuss the **Do's and Don'ts.**

DO:

- Take college prep courses in high school.

- Register for early college and dual college programs.

- Keep track of your Grade Point Average always.

- Volunteer and participate in extracurricular activities if you are a high school student.

- Start looking into colleges no later than your 10th grade year.

- Check with Human Resources at your job for tuition reimbursement programs if you are an Adult learner.

- Tour colleges to get a "real" feel of the campuses.

- Start thinking about what you want to do for a career.

- Look at the guide in chapter 2 to know what you should be doing to fulfill your college goals.

- Take practice PSAT tests.

- Take Straighterline courses.

- Start to research the colleges you may be interested in attending.

- Get a tutor or use online tools for courses you may struggle in.

- Try not to fail any courses.

- Talk to other college students, professors in the field you may be interested in, your teachers, and guidance counselors about college.

- Think about the college's location.

- Review the college's reputation.

- Look at the academic requirements for all colleges you may be interested in.

- Look at the college's diversity or lack of diversity.
- Ask questions.
- Involve parents in your process, but make your own decision based on your research.
- Take the SAT and ACTs.

DO NOT:

- Procrastinate!
- Fail courses.
- Feel ashamed to ask questions.
- Take admissions' counselors' word – research everything for yourself.
- Hire someone to write your college essay (they will not be there when you must write for your courses).
- Ignore deadlines and dates.
- Wait until your senior year to get serious about college.
- Attend a nationally accredited college for any reason.
- Feel forced to enroll in a college. Make your decision promptly.
- Get in trouble with law enforcement.
- Attend a college only because your family and friends attended.
- Let anyone tell you that you are not college material.
- Miss deadlines.
- Sign with the first team if you are an athlete. Research all the schools' graduation rates.

- Enroll in a school because of a full tuition scholarship (right fit socially, academically, and financially.
- Give up (even if you fail a class).
- Take a break from college for more than one semester.

CHAPTER FOURTEEN:

The Real Reasons Why People Don't Graduate from College

I remember my freshman orientation at Norfolk State University. All the transfers and first-year students were packed in Gills Gymnasium. We were busy talking and getting to know one another. Suddenly, a hush fell over the entire Gymnasium. All eyes were glued on the 6'1" tall woman with a stern walk and upright posture. Dean Ruth Jarvis had entered the building. She took the podium and welcomed all of us to Norfolk State University.

She gave a few kinds words, but afterward gave us a jolt of reality. She told us to look to the left, and then look to the right. After we complied, she then told us that one of the individuals would not make it to graduation. I thought that was harsh. However, Dean Jarvis was correct. One of the individuals that I looked in the eye did not make it to graduation. I am going to tell you what Dean Jarvis told me, and the rest of those students in Gills Gymnasium, in 1990. These are the reasons why people do not graduate from college:

- Many students will get pregnant. Trust me, I have seen this over, and over again. Students get a taste of freedom and go wild at college. If you plan to be sexually active in college, please, please use condoms, birth control pills, and PrEP.

- Many students will start using drugs and alcohol. Drug addiction is never good, but it will ruin your college career quickly. Drugs are illegal at many colleges and universities. In addition to this, college is stressful enough. Drugs and overuse of alcohol will affect your academic status in a negative manner.

- Many students will get married and leave college. Please realize that it is okay to find a mate in college, but your primary goal is to learn and get a degree.

- Many students will let their social life take too much of their time. The club scene is not the only place students get overly involved in, but church events as well. Do everything in moderation.

- Many students will not apply themselves and fail.

- Many students will not get support from their family or must attend to family issues and drop out.

- Many students will get homesick and leave.

- Many students will not have enough money to complete school.

- Many students will get sent home for criminal activities.

- Demanding jobs will force some students to quit.

I am sure there are many other reasons why students will not graduate, but these are the usual culprits. Dean Ruth Jarvis was spot on in her assessment.   When I became an academic dean, I saw students dropping out because they just were not prepared for college courses. Some students came from high schools that were very dysfunctional and lacking resources. However, I noticed that some students attended high achieving schools, but did not know how to write a complete sentence. I realized that many of these schools did not want to tarnish their reputations, so they just passed students through to the next grade level and then on to graduation. In other words, they were just "pushed" through the system.

Once again parents, this is why I am such a fan of StraighterLine. You should spend $59.00 - $179.00 on a college course at StraighterLine instead, then spending $1,500.00 per class at a regular college. If you are not sure your son or daughter is ready for college, use StraighterLine to find out. If they pass the class, they can transfer the credit. If they fail the course, you are just out of $59.00. Also, Straighterline only transfers passing courses, so there is no academic penalty for the student.

Remember, college is a serious business. Using this book can help you to find the right college that fits you socially, academically, and financially, which will lead to your being accepted, retained, and lead to your graduation. I hope that this publication increases graduations rates among first-generation students and adult learners.

REFERENCES

Simply College www.simplycollege.net

Khan Academy www.khanacamdemy.com

Crash Course Channel on YouTube

Advance Placement, or AP Courses
https://apstudent.collegeboard.org/home

International Baccalaureate Program https://www.ibo.org

CLEP TEST (College-Level Examination Program
https://clep.collegeboard.org

Straighterline https://www.straighterline.com/

U.S. Dept. of Education https://www.ed.gov/

TRIO https://www2.ed.gov/about/offices/list/ope/trio

Middle States Association of Colleges and Schools
https://www.chea.org/regional-accrediting-organizations#middle-states

New England Association of Schools and Colleges
https://www.chea.org/regional-accrediting-organizations#new-england-institutions

North Central Association of Colleges and Schools (Now known as Higher Learning Commission
https://www.chea.org/regional-accrediting-organizations#north-central

Northwest Commission on Colleges and Universities
http://www.nwccu.org/

Southern Association of Colleges and Schools
https://www.chea.org/regional-accrediting-organizations#southern

Western Association of Schools and Colleges
https://www.chea.org/regional-accrediting-organizations#western-senior

Council for Higher Education Accreditation/International Quality Group
https://www.chea.org/search-institutions

Database of Accredited Postsecondary Institutions and Programs
https://ope.ed.gov/dapip

Distance Education & Training Council (DETC)
https://www.deac.org/

Accrediting Commission of Career Schools and Colleges (ACCSC)
https://www.accsc.org/

Council on Occupational Education (COE)
https://council.org/achieving-accreditation/

Transnational Association of Christian Colleges and Schools, Accreditation Commission
https://www.tracs.org/

Council for Higher Education Accreditation/International Quality Group
https://www.chea.org/programmatic-accrediting-organizations

Report from former Senator Tom Harkins
https://www.help.senate.gov/imo/media/for_profit_report/Contents.pdf

Middle States Commission on Higher Education
https://www.ciachef.edu/accreditation/

Commission on Accrediting of the Association of Theological Schools
http://united.edu/accreditation-association/

GuideStar https://www.guidestar.org/Home.aspx

How to Prepare For a College Interview Blog
https://blog.prepscholar.com/college-interview-questions-you-should-prepare-for

BIBLIOGRAPHY

Aims Community College. (2018). *Appeal of Satisfactory Academic Progress (SAP)*. Retrieved from Aims Community College: https://www.aims.edu/student/finaid/sap.php

Bidwell, A. (2018, January 25). *GAO: Experts Identify Accreditation Challenges With Oversight, Measuring Quality.* Retrieved from National Association of Student Financial Aid Administrators: https://www.nasfaa.org/news-item/14213/GAO_Experts_Identify_Accreditation_Challenges_With_Oversight_Measuring_Quality

Board, T. C. (2011). *Get it Togther for College, 2nd ed.*

Brint, S., & Karabel, J. (1989). *The diverted dream: community colleges and the promise of educational opportunity.* . New York: Oxford University Press.

Council for Higher Education Accreditation. (2015). *Accreditation & Recognition.* Retrieved from About Accreditation : https://www.chea.org/about-accreditation

Counseling, N. A., & Assocation, A. S. (2015). *STATE-BY-STATE STUDENT-TO-COUNSELOR RATIO REPORT 10-YEAR TRENDS* . Arlington, VA; Alexandria, VA: National Association for College Admission Counseling; American School Counseling Assocation.

Cowley, S. (2018, December 6). *For-Profit College Chain Closes, Shutting Out Nearly 20,000 Students.* Retrieved from The New York Times: https://www.nytimes.com/2018/12/06/business/education-corporation-of-america-closing.html

Drury, R. L. (2003). Community Colleges in America: A Historical Perspective . *Inquiry*, 1-6.

Flores, A. (2018, July 3). *The 85 Colleges That Only ACICS Would Accredit.* Retrieved from Center for American Progress: https://www.americanprogress.org/issues/education-postsecondary/news/2018/07/03/453079/85-colleges-acics-accredit/

GetEducated. (2018). *Regional Accreditation vs National Accreditation for Online Colleges.* Retrieved from GetEducated.com: https://www.geteducated.com/regional-vs-national-accreditation-which-is-better-for-online-colleges

Harris, A. (2018, March 25). *Federal Judge Hands a Victory to Embattled Accreditor.* Retrieved from The Chronicle of Higher Education: https://www.chronicle.com/article/Federal-Judge-Hands-a-Victory/242918

International Baccalaureate Organization. (2013, August). *What is IB an education.* Retrieved from International Baccalaureate: https://www.ibo.org/globalassets/what-is-an-ib-education-2017-en.pdf

Johnstone, S. M., Ewell, P., & Paulson, K. (2010, March). *Student Learning as Academic Currency.* Retrieved from American

Council on Education: https://www.acenet.edu/news-room/Pages/Student-Learning-as-Academic-Currency.aspx

Landry, S., & McWhirter, K. (2018). *CLEP Exams: How to Get College Credit & Graduate Faster.* Retrieved from Affordable Colleges Online: https://www.affordablecollegesonline.org/college-resource-center/clep-exam/

Pannoni, A. (2014, September). *Discover the Difference Between AP and IB Courses.* Retrieved from US New and Report: https://www.usnews.com/education/blogs/high-school-notes/2014/09/02/discover-the-difference-between-ap-and-ib-courses

Selingo, J. J. (2015, July 20). *How many colleges and universities do we really need?* . Retrieved from The Washington Post: https://www.washingtonpost.com/news/grade-point/wp/2015/07/20/how-many-colleges-and-universities-do-we-really-need/?noredirect=on&utm_term=.9036f3cbae79

The College Board. (2012). *Choose AP.* Retrieved from College Board, Advanced Placement: http://media.collegeboard.com/homeOrg/content/pdf/12b_6385_AP_IndiaBro_Update_WEB_120816.pdf

US News and Report. (2018). Retrieved from Best Colleges: US News and Report: https://www.usnews.com/best-colleges/byu-3670

Waldman, A. (2015, November 3). *Who Keeps Billions of Taxpayer Dollars Flowing to For-profit Colleges? These Guys.* Retrieved from ProPublica: https://www.propublica.org/article/accreditors-billions-of-taxpayer-dollars-flowing-to-for-profit-colleges

ABOUT THE AUTHOR

Dr. James Wilcox, Jr. is a native of Cocoa, Florida where he attended Rockledge High School, Rockledge, Florida. James served as Academic Dean for Strayer University, San Antonio, Texas and Dayton, OH, for eight years. He was also Director of Student Success for National American University for two years. James has served as an online-professor and brick-and-mortar professor for over ten years. James received his Bachelor of Music emphasis in Media and Master of Arts in Mass Communication degrees from Norfolk State University, Norfolk, Virginia. He earned a Master of Science in Management degree from Strayer University, Washington, D.C. and a Master of Management in e-Marketing degree from National American University, Rapid City, South Dakota. James earned his Doctor of Ministry degree from United Theological Seminary in Dayton, Ohio. Currently, James does public speaking and owns Simply College, for academic advising. James resides in San Antonio, Texas.

SIMPLY COLLEGE

College Made Simple

We are here to help you get there!

Simply College's Mission:

This is why we do what we do!

SIMPLY COLLEGE'S MISSION: *To offer sensible and realistic advice to individuals interested in attending college, while finding colleges that closely fit the individual academically, financially, and socially.*

Time is money and selecting the wrong college could be costly. The staff at Simply College is here to guide you through the college admission process. We make it easy. We make it enjoyable. We make it **SIMPLE**! We will show you how to save money on college tuition. We will help you earn college credits before even stepping foot on a college campus. We will even guide you through the sometimes confusing financial aid process. A small investment in Simply College's advisement program will save you THOUSANDS of dollars in the long run. THE INVESTMENT IS WORTH IT! YOU ARE WORTH IT! INVEST IN YOURSELF!

THE INVESTMENT IS WORTH IT! YOU ARE WORTH IT! INVEST IN YOURSELF!

Our Products and Services

- Dual credit courses and online college courses
- Test evaluation
- Counseling on colleges and universities
- Application seminar
- Financial Aid seminar
- Money management and college scholarships
- High school to college transition seminar
- College requirements
- High school course guidance and assistance
- AP course help
- Online college credits
- Academic assessment
- Parental counseling
- Career services
- Student motivation and benchmark completion

For the adult learner, Simply College will assist you in researching your employer's educational benefits.

- If you have attended college and want to return, Simply College is here to help you!
- If you are a Veteran, Simply College will assist you in selecting a college that understands V.A. benefits.

Simply College will help all students select reputable and regionally accredited colleges and universities. We want to make your process – **SIMPLE!**

Who We Are

About Us

While serving as an academic dean, our founder, Dr. James Wilcox, found himself advising students about college programs they should pursue. Each academic year, students made it a point to find Dr. Wilcox to help them with their academic journey. Dr. Wilcox had an idea! Why not help students before they even get to college! Dr. Wilcox's logic was, it would be a **simple** transition from high school, or the workplace, to college, if students knew the process. From this, Simply College was formed!

Contact Us

Phone: 321-258-6328
Email: dr.jameswilcox@yahoo.com
Web: www.simplycollege.net

SIMPLY COLLEGE
317 HIGHLAND PL
CIBOLO, TX 78108